SCHOLASTIC discover more™

ancient egypt

By Penelope Arlon

Free digital book

Read the strangest and scariest stories about ancient Egyptian mummies in your free digital book.

amazing mummy tales

A digital companion to Ancient Egypt

Download your all-new digital book,

Amazing Mummy Tales

Log on to
www.scholastic.com/discovermore

Enter this special code:

RCHKGMG6PWWF

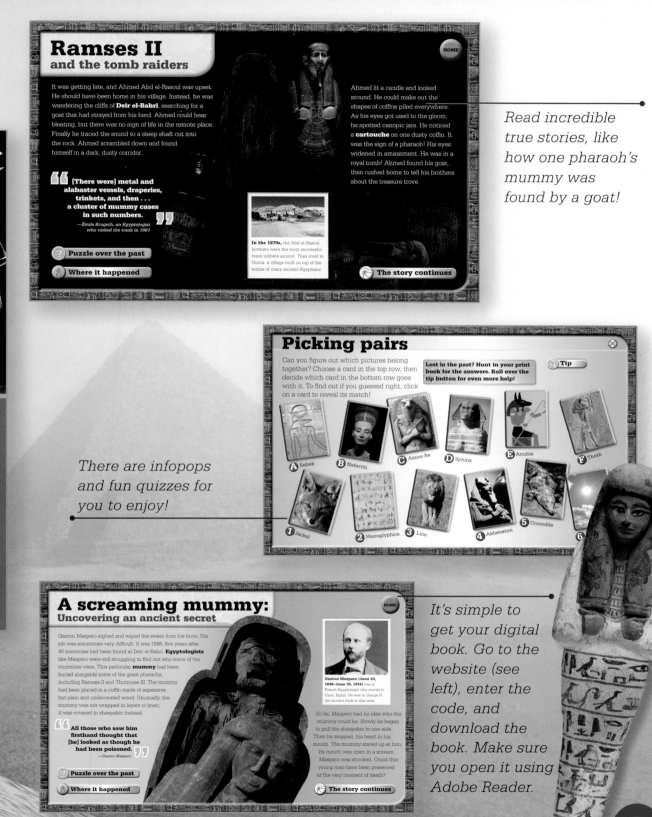

Ramses II
and the tomb raiders

HOME

It was getting late, and Ahmed Abd el-Rasoul was upset. He should have been home in his village. Instead, he was wandering the cliffs of **Deir el-Bahri**, searching for a goat that had strayed from his herd. Ahmed could hear bleating, but there was no sign of life in the remote place. Finally he traced the sound to a steep shaft cut into the rock. Ahmed scrambled down and found himself in a dark, dusty corridor.

> [There were] metal and alabaster vessels, draperies, trinkets, and then . . . a cluster of mummy cases in such numbers.
>
> —Émile Brugsch, an Egyptologist who visited the tomb in 1881

Ahmed lit a candle and looked around. He could make out the shapes of coffins piled everywhere. As his eyes got used to the gloom, he spotted canopic jars. He noticed a **cartouche** on one dusty coffin. It was the sign of a pharaoh! His eyes widened in amazement. He was in a royal tomb! Ahmed found his goat, then rushed home to tell his brothers about the treasure trove.

In the 1870s, the Abd el-Rasoul brothers were the most successful tomb robbers around. They lived in Qurna, a village built on top of the tombs of many ancient Egyptians.

? Puzzle over the past

Where it happened

The story continues

Read incredible true stories, like how one pharaoh's mummy was found by a goat!

Picking pairs

Can you figure out which pictures belong together? Choose a card in the top row, then decide which card in the bottom row goes with it. To find out if you guessed right, click on a card to reveal its match!

Lost in the past? Hunt in your print book for the answers. Roll over the tip button for even more help!

Tip

A Sebek B Nefertiti C Amon-Re D Sphinx E Anubis F Thoth

1 Jackal 2 Hieroglyphics 3 Lion 4 Akhenaton 5 Crocodile 6

There are infopops and fun quizzes for you to enjoy!

A screaming mummy:
Uncovering an ancient secret

HOME

Gaston Maspero sighed and wiped the sweat from his brow. His job was sometimes very difficult. It was 1886, five years after 40 mummies had been found at Deir el-Bahri. **Egyptologists** like Maspero were still struggling to find out who some of the **mummies** were. This particular **mummy** had been buried alongside some of the great pharaohs, including Ramses II and Thutmose III. The mummy had been placed in a coffin made of expensive but plain and undecorated wood. Unusually, the mummy was not wrapped in layers of linen; it was covered in sheepskin instead.

> All those who saw him firsthand thought that [he] looked as though he had been poisoned.
>
> —Gaston Maspero

Gaston Maspero (June 23, 1846–June 30, 1916) was a French Egyptologist who moved to Cairo, Egypt. He was in charge of the ancient finds in that area.

So far, Maspero had no idea who the mummy could be. Slowly he began to pull the sheepskin to one side. Then he stopped, his heart in his mouth. The mummy stared up at him. Its mouth was open in a scream. Maspero was shocked. Could this young man have been preserved at the very moment of death?

? Puzzle over the past

Where it happened

The story continues

It's simple to get your digital book. Go to the website (see left), enter the code, and download the book. Make sure you open it using Adobe Reader.

3

Consultant:
Loretta Kilroe
Literacy Consultant:
Barbara Russ,
21st Century Community
Learning Center Director for
Winooski (Vermont) School District

Library of Congress Cataloging-in-Publication
Data Available

ISBN 978-0-545-62739-9

10 9 8 7 6 5 4 3 2 1   14 15 16 17 18

Printed in Singapore   46
First edition, July 2014

Scholastic is constantly working to lessen the
environmental impact of our manufacturing
processes. To view our industry-leading
paper procurement policy, visit
www.scholastic.com/paperpolicy.

Contents

Discovering ancient Egypt

Everyday life

Discovering ancient Egypt

Ancient Egypt flourished along the banks of the Nile River for more than 3,000 years. Today, the Pyramids of Giza stretch high into the sky behind modern Cairo. They are a world-famous reminder that ancient Egypt was one of the greatest civilizations ever.

Ancient Egypt

Ancient Egypt was one of the first and most incredible civilizations on Earth. It produced amazing art, huge buildings, and great rulers.

Written language

Ancient Egyptian was one of the first languages in the world to be written down.

Pharaoh

The pharaoh was the king of Egypt. He organized the government, the army, and building projects.

falcon sculpture

All the cities of ancient Egypt were

Farming

The Egyptians invented smart farming methods that are still used in some places today.

Precious stones were used in trade.

Buildings

The Egyptians were outstanding builders. The 4,500-year-old pyramids are still among the most impressive buildings ever created.

The Egyptians are famous for the way they buried their dead.

The Egyptians believed in many gods and goddesses.

built on the banks of the Nile River.

Nile empire

Much of northeast Africa is desert. The area around the Nile River is the only land fertile enough to grow food. The entire ancient Egyptian civilization grew up along the river's banks. Even today, 95 percent of Egyptians live beside the Nile!

Black land

Ancient Egyptians named their country for the Nile. They called it Kemet, which means "black land," because of the dark, fertile mud on the riverbanks.

EUROPE

ASIA

area shown
at right

AFRICA

The Great Pyramid of Giza is a pharaoh's tomb.

The Valley of the Kings contains hidden tombs.

This temple was built by a female pharaoh, Hatshepsut

Abu Simbel was built by the pharaoh Ramses II.

Heracleion

Mediterranean Sea

LOWER EGYPT

KEY
- ● Famous structure
- ● City or village

Memphis

pyramids at Saqqara

Akhetaton

Nile River

Red Sea

Divided land

Ancient Egypt was divided into two regions. Lower Egypt was in the north, where the Nile River flowed into the Mediterranean Sea. Upper Egypt was in the south. During much of Egypt's ancient history, these areas were one united country, ruled by one pharaoh.

Builders lived in this village, called Deir el-Medina.

Thebes

The Nubian and Egyptian civilizations flourished at the same time. They often invaded each other's territories.

UPPER EGYPT

NUBIA

Karnak was a temple area with many buildings.

How do we know so much about ancient Egypt? Tombs from that time have been found and opened. Some are packed with mummies and the possessions of the dead.

DNA is a substance found in everyone's cells.

All wrapped up!

We can study very lifelike remains of ancient people. The Egyptians mummified, or preserved, bodies after death.

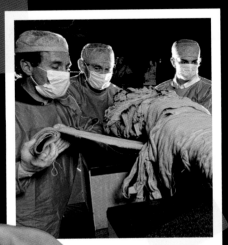

Mummy studies

Egyptologists can take a tiny piece of a mummy and test its DNA. This can tell us who the mummy was related to, since people in the same family have similar DNA.

Jewels are sometimes found inside a mummy's linen wrappings.

Tomb treasures

The most famous tomb find of all time happened in 1922, when the tomb of the pharaoh Tutankhamen was discovered. Inside were thrones, four chariots, statues, jewels, furniture, bread, perfume jars, and his pillow!

▶▶▶ **Find out more** about making mummies on pages 62–63.

A mummy's hair shows us ancient hairstyles!

RECENT FINDS

DONKEY DISCOVERY

In 1996, a donkey got its leg trapped in a hole at the Bahariya Oasis. The hole turned out to be the entrance to a vast tomb. It was named the Valley of the Golden Mummies.

OLDEST PAPERS

The Egyptians used a kind of paper called papyrus (see page 22). The oldest known papyrus was found in 2013—it showed that workers received bread and beer.

MURDER!

The mummy of Ramses III was scanned in 2012. This revealed that his throat had been slashed. He had been murdered!

Tomb treasures

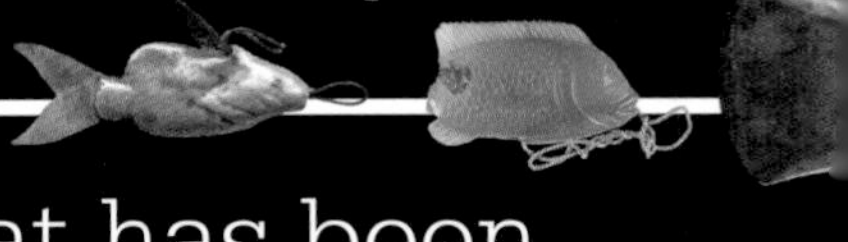
fish pendants

Imagine opening an Egyptian tomb that has been closed for 3,000 years. Here are some of the things that you might find inside. Watch out for mummies!

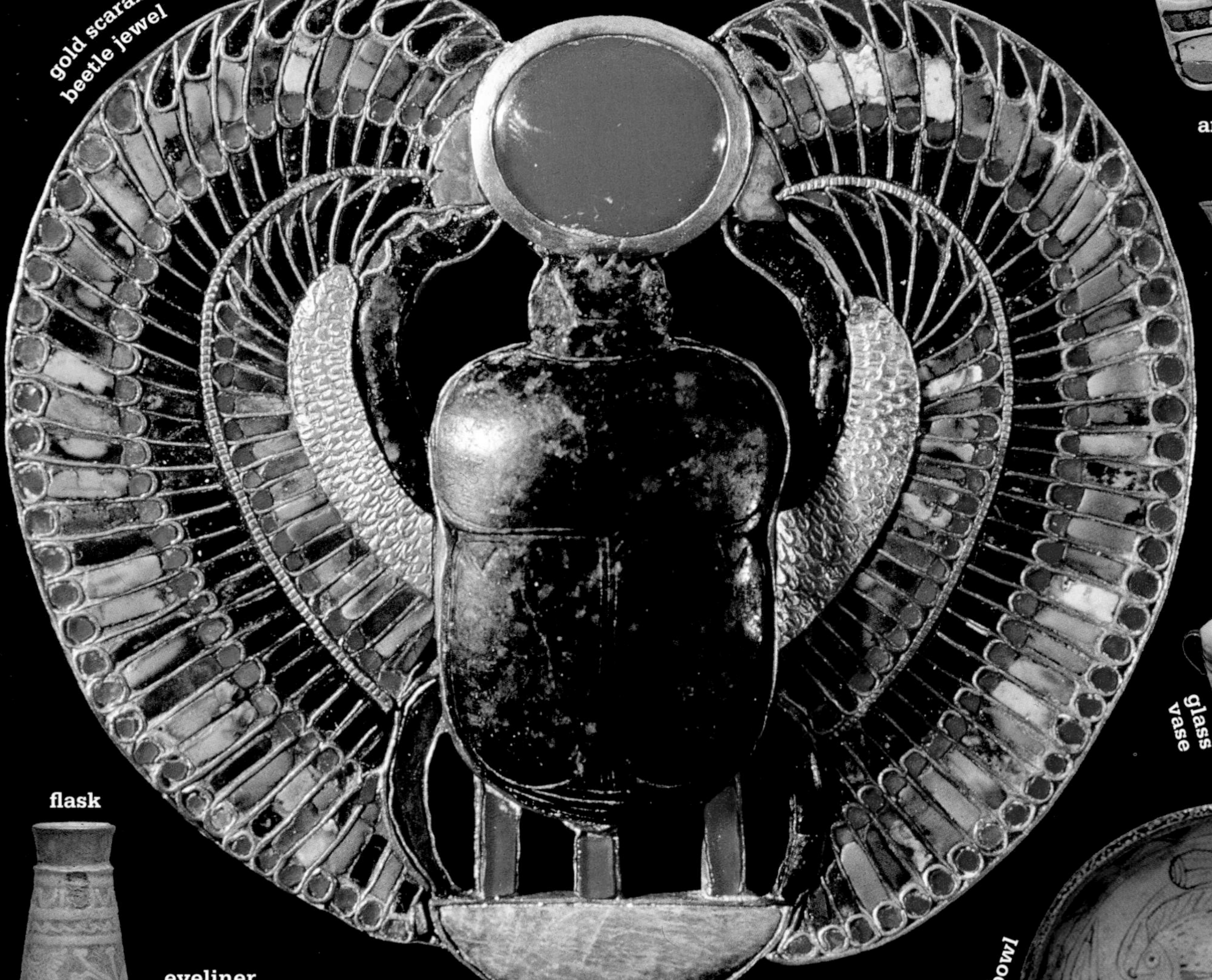
gold scarab beetle jewel

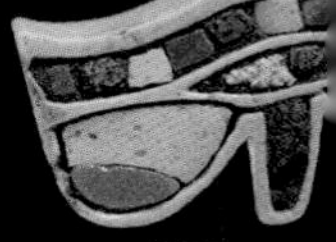
eye amulet

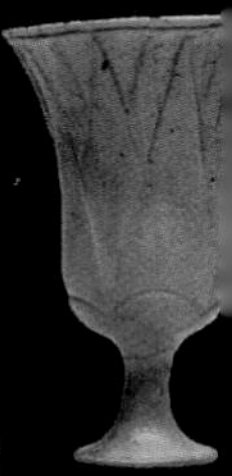
drinkin cup

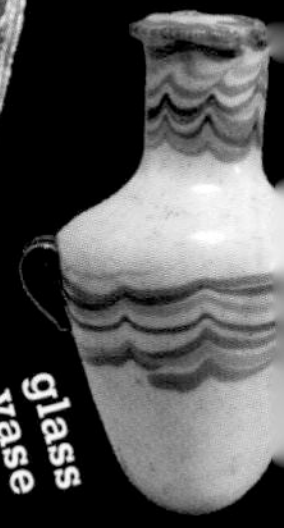
glass vase

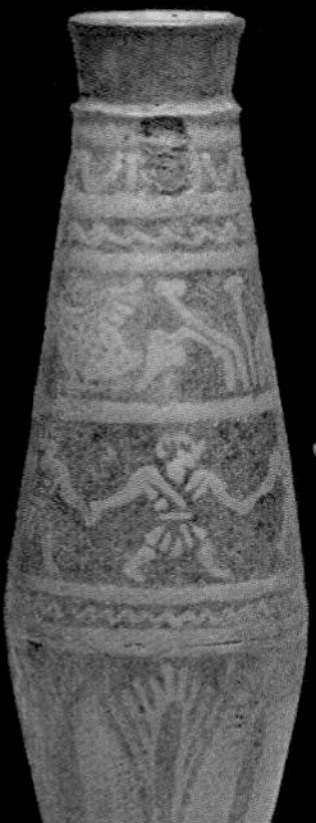
flask

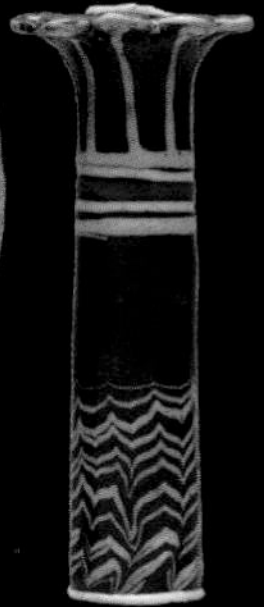
eyeliner pot

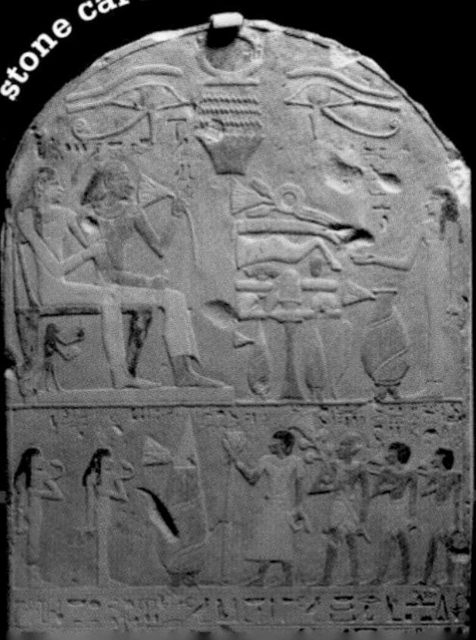
stone carving

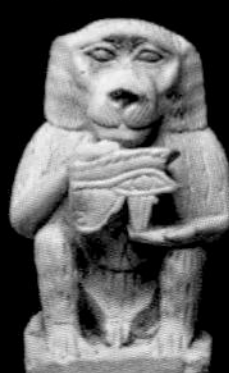
baboon amulet

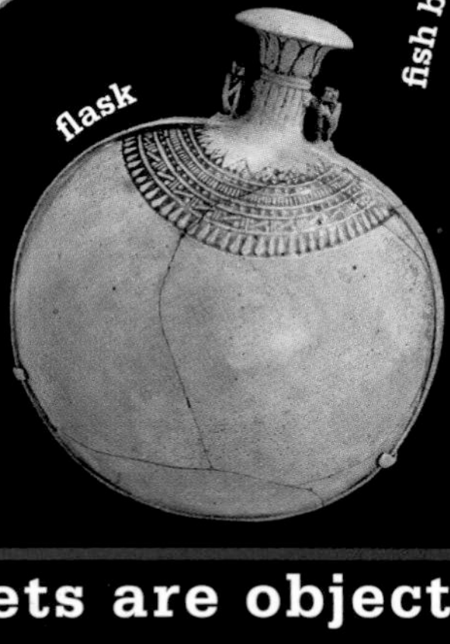
flask

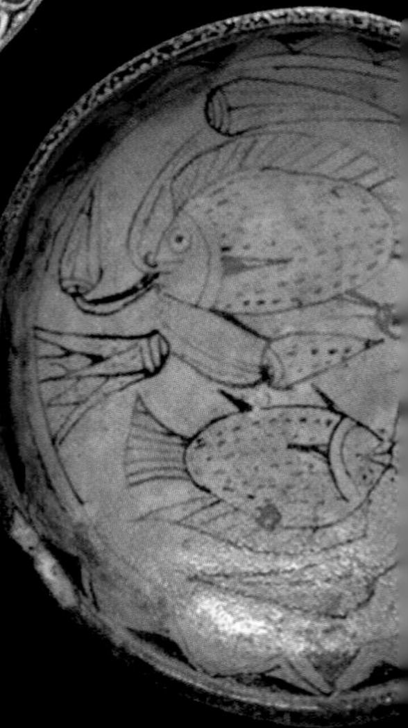
fish bowl

Amulets are objects carried for

god amulet

winged beetle necklace

ibis pendant

lion pendant

bead

glass pot

dagger

double jar

cheetah necklace

scarab amulet (top and bottom)

model boat

ax

wooden statues

mummy

ax

wooden comb

makeup jar

senet board and pieces

baboon mummy's coffin

mummy mask

frog rings

cat mummy

good luck.

LORD CARNARVON

The problem with putting all your valuable possessions in tombs is that people can break inside and take them! In ancient Egyptian times, raiders stole all the priceless treasures from the tombs inside pyramids. So people started to bury their dead deep inside mountains. But the raiders still found them.

Lord Carnarvon and Carter

Fast-forward to 1922. Many people hoped that the greatest tombs were still waiting to be discovered. Lord Carnarvon, a wealthy Englishman, was on an archaeological dig in the Valley of the Kings with Egyptologist Howard Carter. (Actually, Lord Carnarvon sat in a screened cage, to avoid dust and flies, and let his team do all the digging!) The team had found some steps leading to a sealed door. They broke in, and found themselves in the tomb of the pharaoh Tutankhamen.

Highclere Castle, Lord Carnarvon's home in England

The rooms were full of amazing treasures, beautiful wall paintings, and even Tutankhamen's shoes! Beneath a gold mask lay the mummy of the pharaoh himself. His treasures now tour the world for everyone to see.

the treasures, exactly as they were found in 1922

Tutankhamen's death mask

THE CURSE OF THE MUMMY?

Some say that a deadly curse is unleashed on those who disturb Tutankhamen. Lord Carnarvon died from an infected mosquito bite soon after the tomb was found. It was recently discovered that Tutankhamen himself may have died of malaria—a disease spread by mosquitoes. Is that weird or what?

The lost city

For centuries, there were rumors of an Egyptian city of great wealth called Heracleion. But no one knew exactly where it had been located. Recently, though, Egyptologists discovered an entire city where the Nile meets the Mediterranean Sea—underwater! It was once the port of Heracleion, but it was flooded by the sea over time.

Divers have found temples, ships, giant statues,

jewelry, and much more lying at the bottom of the sea.

Time line of Egypt

Ancient Egypt lasted for 3,000 years. Follow the river to read about power and progress and about darker times.

People began farming along the Nile's banks about 7,300 years ago

5300–3000 BCE

Middle Kingdom

Egypt was reunited by the pharaoh Mentuhotep II, and Thebes became the capital. It was a peaceful period in Egypt, and the arts flourished.

This was an unsettled time in Egypt—tales tell of "70 kings in 70 days." There was drought and strife.

2160–2055 BCE

gold artwork

2055–1650 BCE

This was another unsettled period. The Hyksos people, from Asia, took over Lower Egypt.

1650–1550 BCE

Tutankhamen
(ruled 1336–1327 BCE)

New Kingdom

This was a time of wealth and power. Strong rulers expanded the kingdom to the south and into the Middle East.

1550–1069 BCE

step pyramid at Saqqara   **Pyramids of Giza**

Ancient Egypt began

In 3000 BCE, the first king, Menes, united Upper and Lower Egypt. About 2650 BCE, the first pyramid was built at Saqqara, near Memphis, the capital at the time.

3000–2686 BCE

Old Kingdom

Egypt expanded its trade and influence. The Pyramids of Giza were built during this "age of the pyramids."

2686–2160 BCE

Cleopatra

Egypt was again divided. It was taken over first by the Libyans, from the west, and later by the Nubians, from the south.

Greek helmet

Later periods

Egypt was conquered by many nations, including Assyria and Persia. In 332 BCE, Alexander the Great of Greece took over Egypt.

1069–664 BCE

664–30 BCE

Cleopatra was the last pharaoh of Egypt. In 30 BCE, Egypt fell under Roman rule.

Ancient inventions

The Egyptians invented some pretty cool stuff, some of which we still use today. Luckily, though, we make our toothpaste differently now!

eyeliner...

Today, tractors pull plows!

Paper today is made from wood pulp.

OX-DRAWN PLOW

FUN FACT

The Egyptians realized that they could use animals (instead of themselves) to pull farm equipment. This made farmers' lives much easier.

WHEN?

About 2500 BCE

This farm painting was found in the tomb of Sennutem.

EYE MAKEUP

FUN FACT

Ancient Egyptian men and women loved to look beautiful. They ground up lead to make black eyeliner. Egyptians still use this mixture today.

WHEN?

About 4000 BCE

Egyptians kept makeup in boxes, just like we do.

PAPER

FUN FACT

The first kind of paper, called papyrus, was made in ancient Egypt. Writing on paper was much quicker than carving symbols into stone!

WHEN?

About 2560 BCE

Papyrus is a reed that grows by the Nile River.

WRITING

FUN FACT

One of the earliest written languages was invented in Egypt. People drew little pictures called hieroglyphics to stand for words.

WHEN?

About 3000 BCE

For a long time, we didn't know what hieroglyphics said!

The Egyptians invented lots of medicines. Some are

Some of the early locks were as effective as locks today.

Today, many wigs are made of man-made materials.

We still organize our lives around the calendar.

The Egyptians may have used frayed twigs as toothbrushes.

DOOR LOCK

FUN FACT

Egyptians invented locks and keys as a way to try to stop tomb raiders. One of the earliest locks was 2 feet (0.6 m) long!

WHEN?
About 4000 BCE

The locks were known as bolt-and-latch locks.

WIG

FUN FACT

The Egyptians used razors to shave their heads and faces. Then they put on the first wigs and fake beards!

WHEN?
About 2600 BCE

The first wigs were made of real hair and sheep's wool.

CALENDAR

FUN FACT

The first calendar had three seasons, each with four months of 30 days. That added up to 360 days. An extra 5 days were religious holidays.

WHEN?
About 3000 BCE

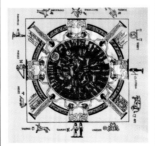

The months were known by numbers rather than names.

TOOTHPASTE

FUN FACT

To help prevent tooth decay, ancient Egyptians invented the first toothpaste. They even made a breath freshener out of honey and cinnamon.

WHEN?
About 1500 BCE

Toothpaste was made of burned eggshells, ashes, or powdered ox hooves—yuck!

still used—but not ground-up mouse to cure coughs!

Everyday life

Life was good for ancient Egyptians. They had an organized government, enough food to eat, and plenty of skilled work to do. This amazing carving is from the back of the pharaoh Tutankhamen's golden throne. It shows the pharaoh and his queen, wearing clothes and wigs typical of wealthy Egyptians.

River

...ancient Egyptians a rich life. It
...shwater, good soil for farming,
...ay through the entire kingdom.

Riverbank farming

The Nile floods every year, leaving fertile soil on its banks. The banks are perfect places to grow crops. Here, farmers are carrying barley.

Boats were made using only wood and ropes, not nails.

Nile travel

The Egyptians didn't build roads. They didn't need to—the Nile was their highway. They made canals as side streets and used only boats for transport.

This boat used oars or sails, depending on which way the wind was blowing.

Nile trade

Egypt was the richest country in the ancient world. Egyptians traded their gold, papyrus, linen, and ornaments for other metals, wood, and food.

The Nile River is the longest river in the

Three seasons

Wheat and barley were the main grains.

Akhet
(July–November)
When the river flooded, people couldn't farm. Instead, they built pyramids, temples, and tombs.

Peret
(November–March)
The floods receded and left behind rich soil. The farmers returned to plow the land and sow seeds.

Shomu
(March–July)
Grain was ready for harvesting. Farmers cut their crops with sickles.

Canals were created to link buildings, like temples, to the river.

Busy, busy river
The Nile would have been packed with boats—small fishing boats, sailboats, huge trade barges, and the pharaoh's boat, decorated with carvings and gold.

world. It is 4,132 miles (6,650 km) long!

Magic and mystery

The ancient Egyptians worshipped many gods and goddesses who they thought helped them in everyday life. They also believed in magic and spells.

Sekhmet, warrior goddess

Gods

Each god represented an object or activity. Most of them were associated with an animal and were often shown with an animal head or as an animal.

Amon-Re, the sun god

Apis, god of strength

Sacred cats

Bastet was linked with cats, so Egyptians mummified cats as offerings to her. There were 300,000 cat mummies in the temple at Bubastis!

This magical carving protected against crocodiles.

Magic

People believed that magic brought them good or bad luck. They carried good-luck charms around with them and called on magicians to ward off bad luck.

Medicine

Egyptians believed that illness was caused by evil spirits. Honey or garlic was given as treatment, and spells were chanted to aid recovery.

Khons, god of the moon.....

Mut, protector of the pharaoh

Taurt, goddess of childbirth.....

Magic wands

In times of need, magicians chanted spells and used ivory wands to draw circles of protection around people.

Find out more about belief in the afterlife on pages 60–61.

This magic wand shows protecting spirits and gods. It is made of a hippo tusk.

Gods and goddesses

There were as many as 2,000 Egyptian gods and goddesses. That's a lot to remember! Here are some of the main gods.

Isis was one of the best-loved goddesses.

Anubis is shown with the head of a jackal, since jackals were often found around cemeteries.

Hathor was often thought of as the mother of the pharaoh. She is shown with cow ears.

Isis

SIGNIFICANCE:
Goddess of children and magic; the mother goddess
SYMBOL:
A kite (a bird of prey)

Anubis

SIGNIFICANCE:
God of magic, mummies, and the dead
SYMBOL:
A jackal

Hathor

SIGNIFICANCE:
Goddess of love and joy; wife of Horus
SYMBOL:
A cow

Amon-Re

SIGNIFICANCE:
The sun god; the most important god
SYMBOL:
The sun

Thoth gave the Egyptians writing, medicine, and mathematics.

Osiris is often shown with a high crown of two ostrich feathers.

Egyptians believed that the pharaoh was the "living Horus."

Thoth

SIGNIFICANCE:
God of the moon and wisdom

SYMBOL:
A baboon or an ibis (a wading bird)

Horus

SIGNIFICANCE:
God of the sky and protector of Egypt; king of the gods; son of Osiris and Isis

SYMBOL:
A falcon

Osiris

SIGNIFICANCE:
Ruler of the underworld

SYMBOL:
A mummified man

e was swallowed by Nut, the
ky goddess, every night and
eborn every morning.

Sebek

SIGNIFICANCE:
God of water and the Nile

SYMBOL:
A crocodile

The temples at Karnak

The Egyptians built temples as homes for the gods. They are some of the most incredible buildings ever constructed on our planet.

Karnak

The temples at Karnak are enormous. The main temple—dedicated to Amon-Re—could hold about 35 soccer fields! Experts think that 80,000 people worked there during the reign of Ramses II.

A canal ran from the Nile to Karnak so that the pharaoh

Temple complex

The Karnak complex was (and still is) the biggest religious center in the world. It was built over a period of 1,500 years and covers more than 200 acres.

Sphinx avenue

Ramses II built an avenue lined with sphinxes that led to the entrance of the main temple. Each statue bears his name

The oracle

Gods were there to solve problems and answer questions for people. A priest asked a god a question, then passed on the answer. This was known as consulting an oracle.

could arrive there by boat.

The pharaoh

statue of Ramses II
found at Abu Simbel

cobra

A pharaoh ruled Egypt. But he was more than a king—to the people, he was a god. He had absolute power, but it was his duty to be honest and fair.

Procession for a pharaoh

A pharaoh made laws, defended the land, and built temples. People even thought that the pharaoh could make it rain! The tomb painting below shows a procession of people paying tribute to Ramses II.

Find out more about Ramses II at war on pages 42–43.

Everyone had to kiss the ground beneath the pharaoh's feet.

During the Heb-Sed festival, a

Ankh

The ankh symbol was the key of life. It showed that the holder had the power to give life or take it away. Pharaohs were often seen holding it in carvings.

Pharaoh training

A pharaoh would often choose his child to become the next pharaoh. The child would be trained from birth in warfare, sports, and leadership.

SPOT A PHARAOH

COBRA

In art, a pharaoh commonly has a cobra head on his crown. This represents the pharaoh's protector.

HEADDRESS

A pharaoh sometimes wore a nemes, a striped headdress, with a cobra on it.

COLORED CROWN

In early periods, the pharaoh wore the red crown of Lower Egypt, the white crown of Upper Egypt, or both combined into one crown. By the time of the New Kingdom, the pharaoh wore a bright blue crown.

Until the later periods, Egypt did not use money. People paid for things with goods or labor. They had to give part of whatever they grew or made to the pharaoh.

These men are slaves who will be offered to the pharaoh. Their hands are tied together.

pharaoh had to prove his strength by racing a bull!

Great pharaohs

There were about 330 pharaohs, who ruled over 3,000 years. Here are a few famous ones.

This statue of Djoser is the oldest known life-size statue in the world.

This statue is the smallest Egyptian royal statue ever found.

Pepi II is shown here as a child with his mother, Ankhesenpepi II.

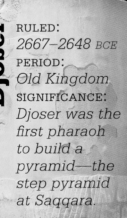

Djoser

RULED:
2667–2648 BCE

PERIOD:
Old Kingdom

SIGNIFICANCE:
Djoser was the first pharaoh to build a pyramid—the step pyramid at Saqqara.

Khufu

RULED:
2589–2566 BCE

PERIOD:
Old Kingdom

SIGNIFICANCE:
Khufu built the Great Pyramid of Giza, one of the Seven Wonders of the Ancient World.

Pepi II

RULED:
2278–2184 BCE

PERIOD:
Old Kingdom

SIGNIFICANCE:
Pepi II had the longest reign in the world—ever! He ruled for 94 years.

The 330 pharaohs were divided into about 30 different

Mentuhotep II reunited Egypt after the First Intermediate period. He was the first pharaoh of the Middle Kingdom.

Thutmose III was too young to reign when his father died. His stepmother, Hatshepsut, ruled in his place.

When Hatshepsut died, Thutmose III took back sole control of the throne.

Mentuhotep II

RULED:
2055–2004 BCE
PERIOD:
Middle Kingdom
SIGNIFICANCE:
Mentuhotep II built a glorious temple tomb on the west bank of the Nile.

Thutmose III

RULED:
1479–1425 BCE
PERIOD:
New Kingdom
SIGNIFICANCE:
Thutmose III was a great military ruler. He may have conquered 350 cities!

Hatshepsut

RULED:
1473–1458 BCE
PERIOD:
New Kingdom
SIGNIFICANCE:
Hatshepsut was one of the few women to rule Egypt.

families, known as dynasties.

Amenhotep III built himself the biggest temple tomb ever found.

Akhenaton changed his name from Amenhotep IV.

Tutankhamen took the throne when he was 10 and died when he was 19.

Amenhotep III

RULED:
1390–1352 BCE

PERIOD:
New Kingdom

SIGNIFICANCE:
Amenhotep III ruled peacefully when Egypt was at the height of its artistic and political power.

Akhenaton

RULED:
1352–1336 BCE

PERIOD:
New Kingdom

SIGNIFICANCE:
Akhenaton worshipped the sun disk god, Aton, and outlawed the worship of other gods.

Tutankhamen

RULED:
1336–1327 BCE

PERIOD:
New Kingdom

SIGNIFICANCE:
Tutankhamen was buried in an amazing tomb full of treasures after reigning for only nine years.

***Pharaoh* means "great house" and originally referred to**

Ramses II is often referred to as Ramses the Great.

Alexander built the city of Alexandria and made it the capital of Egypt.

Cleopatra was regarded as a great beauty.

Ramses II

RULED:
1279–1213 BCE

PERIOD:
New Kingdom

SIGNIFICANCE:
Ramses II was a great military leader. He also built the temples at Abu Simbel.

Alexander the Great

RULED:
332–323 BCE

PERIOD:
Hellenistic period

SIGNIFICANCE:
Alexander the Great defeated the Persian Empire and conquered Egypt.

Cleopatra VII

RULED:
51–30 BCE

PERIOD:
Ptolemaic period

SIGNIFICANCE:
Cleopatra was the last pharaoh of Egypt.

the royal palace. Hatshepsut changed it to mean "king."

AKHENATON

symbol for Aton ....

Most pharaohs behaved themselves, and Egypt enjoyed a fairly stable history. But in 1352 BCE, Amenhotep IV took control—and during his 16-year reign, he caused chaos.

Amenhotep IV faced few challenges, because previous pharaohs had left Egypt wealthy and peaceful. So he decided to leave his mark on religion. He forebade the worship of the old gods and declared that Aton, the sun disk god (not Amon-Re, the sun god), was the only god. He changed his own name to Akhenaton, closed all the temples, and built a new city called Akhetaton, naming it the new capital of Egypt. All these actions made him very unpopular with his people.

Because Akhenaton was so focused on religion, he

Akhenaton demanded a new style of art that depicted people with long faces and droopy bellies.

40

didn't pay enough attention to his empire's security. Hittites from the north started stealing parts of Egypt. When Akhenaton died, his 10-year-old son, Tutankhaten, took over. Later pharaohs tried to erase Akhenaton from history by destroying his art.

Akhenaton had many wives, but Nefertiti was his favorite—and the most beautiful.

Akhenaton and Nefertiti ····

Nefertiti ······

TUTANKHAMEN

Tutankhaten returned Egypt's capital to Thebes, restored the old gods, and changed his name to Tutankhamen. Egypt had returned to its old ways, but it would never be as powerful as it once had been. Tutankhamen died when he was only 19 years old. He is most famous for his amazing tomb (see pages 16–17).

Warriors

Strong military forces, led by the pharaoh, were made up of well-trained foot soldiers, charioteers, and sailors. Working together, they defended Egypt and conquered nearby lands.

Fighting leader

Ramses II was one of the greatest warrior pharaohs. This painting shows him leading the Egyptians in a battle against the Nubians. Ramses also famously defeated the Hittites at the Battle of Kadesh.

Ramses II drives his horse and chariot into battle.

Left, right, left . . .

Army life was tough. Soldiers had to march hundreds of miles. These model soldiers were found in a tomb.

In times of peace,

Weapons of war

Daggers
Deadly metal swords and daggers were used in hand-to-hand fighting.

Bows and arrows
The Egyptians could shoot arrows over 600 feet (180 m), killing enemies from far away.

Axes
Axes could be used at close range, or they could be thrown.

Ramses's sons follow him. A chariot usually held two people—one to drive and one to shoot.

Ramses has won the battle, so the defeated Nubians bring gold, treasures, exotic animals, and food as tributes.

Axes were excellent at chopping through leather shields.

soldiers built temples and tombs.

Writing

The Egyptians were among the earliest people to write. They drew hieroglyphics, which are pictures that represent sounds and objects.

The Rosetta Stone

For many centuries, no one could read hieroglyphics. Then, in 1799, the Rosetta Stone was found. It has the same words written three times: in ancient Greek, hieroglyphics, and another script. Scholars compared the hieroglyphics to the Greek and translated them.

hieroglyphics

Pens were reeds dipped in black or red ink.

Paper and ink

Paper was made from papyrus reeds. Strips of reed were laid crisscross on a frame and flattened under weights.

ancient Greek

Hieroglyphics

Some hieroglyphics represent sounds that are quite similar to our alphabet sounds today. Here are the hieroglyphics closest to our letters. Now you can write a message in hieroglyphics!

papyrus

a b c d e f

g h i j k l

m n o p q

r s t u v

w x y z

Translate this!

(Answer on page 80.)

Home life

Wealthy Egyptians lived in large houses, but most workers lived in tightly packed villages. Tomb paintings show that they enjoyed family life.

Working village

These houses are in the village of Deir el-Medina. Builders who worked in the Valley of the Kings lived here. The houses are made of mud.

About 68 houses were found in the village.

wooden toe strap

Walk like an Eygptian!

We know that the Egyptians had good doctors—they even made fake toes! This wooden toe, found on a mummy, is the earliest prosthetic (artificial) body part ever discovered!

Egyptian children played with many toys: little clay

unusual pet!

This wooden doll has beaded hair.

Family

This royal tomb builder is with his wife, son, and grandchildren, who are playing with pet birds. They all lived together.

Shady gardens

Larger houses had plant-filled gardens. Wealthy people liked to keep cool in freshwater pools.

Song and dance

Scenes on the walls of tombs show that the Egyptians loved to party! They played music and danced at festivals.

Toys and games

Egyptians had many fun activities. Here, Queen Nefertiti is playing a board game called senet. Turn the page to learn how to play it!

animals, **spinning tops, balls, and board games.**

Senet is one of the oldest board games known. Nobody is quite sure how it was originally played, but this way is fun!

The board

The board has 30 squares. There are 2 players, each with 5 pieces that start in the positions shown. The first player to get all his or her pieces past 30 wins!

Sticks

Egyptians used 4 sticks instead of dice. One side of each stick was patterned; the other was blank. Make your own sticks, and throw them all on each turn.

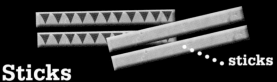

sticks

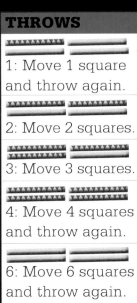

THROWS

1: Move 1 square and throw again.

2: Move 2 squares.

3: Move 3 squares.

4: Move 4 squares and throw again.

6: Move 6 squares and throw again.

1 player 1's pieces

2 player 2's pieces

3

4

5

20

19

18

17

16

21

22

23

24

25

Are you ready to play? Make your own board and

The rules

- *Throw the sticks. Move one of your pieces the number of squares you threw.*
- *If your opponent has a piece on the square that you want to land on, that piece and your piece trade squares.*
- *You can't land on one of your own pieces. Only one piece can be in a square.*
- *If your opponent has two pieces next to each other, you can't trade squares with either of them.*

- *If your opponent has three pieces next to each other, you can't pass them.*
- *15, 26, 28, and 29 are safe squares. No piece on them can be swapped.*
- *If you can't move any of your pieces forward, move one piece backward.*
- *If you can't move at all, you skip a turn.*
- *If you are sent to the Ankh and it is occupied, go to the closest square behind it.*

SPECIAL SQUARES

 Ankh: Safe square. Your piece cannot be moved.

 House of Happiness: Safe square.

 House of Water: Go back to the Ankh.

 House of Three Truths: You MUST throw a 2 to move.

 Eye of Horus: You MUST throw a 1 to move.

sticks, choose your pieces, and give it a try. Good luck!

The hunt

Egyptians loved to hunt, for sport as well as for food. This painting was found on the wall of the tomb of a wealthy scribe named Nebamun.

Nebamun was a nobleman who lived in ancient Egypt around 1350 BCE. In this scene, he is shown hunting for birds.

The Egyptians trained cats to help them hunt. Nebamun's cat would catch birds and bring them back to him.

Ducks were very common on the banks of the Nile and were hunted for food.

Nebamun's boat was made from bundles of papyrus reeds tied together.

Colored paints were made from soot,

A throwing stick was used to hunt birds. It could also be used as a weapon in battle.

Nebamun is shown standing with his shoulders facing front and his head turned to the side. All Egyptian figures were painted in this position.

Wearing jewels and a cone of perfumed wax on her head, Nebamun's wife is dressed for a banquet!

Nebamun's daughter has a sidelock of hair. Children were always painted with this hairstyle.

crushed rocks, or plants, mixed with egg.

The beauty salon

Ancient Egyptians loved dressing up. They wore spectacular jewels, beautiful clothes, and lots of makeup—even the men! Beauty was very important.

Jewelry was made of gold, silver, beads, and precious stones.

Wig style

Egyptians thought that showing your own hair, including beards, looked awful! Instead, they shaved their heads and wore wigs. The wigs were held on their heads with beeswax.

hoop earrings

MAKEUP BAG

Priests and women used tweezers to remove hair.

Mirrors were made of polished bronze.

Wigs were brushed with wooden combs.

Hairpins held elaborate hairstyles in place.

Bronze or copper razors were used to get rid of extra hair.

Green eye paint was made from crushed malachite.

Cheeks were reddened with crushed red metal.

Glittering jewels

No Egyptian outfit was quite finished without some chunky jewelry. Egyptians wore rings, necklaces, bracelets, and earrings. Some pieces, such as this scarab jewel, were believed to bring good luck.

Cones of scented animal fat were melted to make a nice smell!

.... **perfume cone**

Eye makeup

Makeup was important to both men and women. The main type of makeup was black eye paint.

Pleated clothes

Clothes were made of linen. Men wore wraparound skirts, and women wore beautifully pleated dresses.

A necklace of meteorites—rocks from space—has been found!

HATSHEPSUT

Even though the wives of pharaohs were greatly respected as queens, it was very rare for a woman to become a pharaoh herself. One of the few exceptions was Hatshepsut, who reigned from 1473 to 1458 BCE. She wore a crown and even a fake beard!

Hatshepsut's temple at Deir el-Bahri

When Hatshepsut's husband, Thutmose II, died, his son, Thutmose III (by another royal wife), was too young to reign. So Hatshepsut claimed the throne as her own. She was a powerful ruler. She led a famous expedition

gold

the obelisk Hatshepsut built at Karnak

Hatshepsut

to the land of Punt, returning with gold and treasures.

Hatshepsut disappeared mysteriously. Was she killed by her stepson, eager to regain the throne? When Thutmose III was pharaoh, he had Hatshepsut's name removed from all temples and her mummy moved to a lesser tomb.

This statue of Hatshepsut is at her huge temple at Deir el-Bahri, near the Valley of the Kings.

a liver

WHAT REMAINS?

Hapshepsut's liver was found in a canopic jar in her tomb. Her mummy, though, had been moved to her nurse's tomb. It has only recently been confirmed, using DNA tests, that the liver and the mummy are both hers.

Food and drink

Ancient Egyptians ate very well—they loved feasting! When the Nile flooded successfully, there was plenty of food.

Bread and beer

Bread and beer, made from wheat and barley, were a big part of everyone's diet. Beer was safer to drink than water, which could be dirty. There was even a goddess of beer, Tenenet.

Terrible toothache

A bit of sand was added to grain to help grind it for bread. This was very bad for the teeth. Studies of mummies have shown that toothaches were common.

Fresh fruit and veggies

Fruit and vegetables were grown on the banks of the Nile.

bread

onion

garlic

pomegranates

figs

dates

Two bakeries have been found near Giza. They would

Ancient Egyptians had no knives or forks. They ate everything with their fingers!

Geese

There were no chickens in ancient Egypt. But geese and other waterfowl were kept for meat and eggs.

Cattle

Cattle were used for labor and food. When farmers had to transport cattle across the Nile, they chanted spells to keep them safe from crocodiles.

Fish

The Nile held many fish. But fishermen had to watch out for dangerous hippos!

.melons

fish •........

The Egyptians ate hedgehogs, cooked in clay to remove the spines.

have produced bread and beer for pyramid workers.

Afterlife

The ancient Egyptians believed that they would pass into an afterlife when they died. But they could only do so if they had behaved well on Earth. Here, the god Anubis weighs a person's heart against the feather of truth.

Journey to the afterlife

When a person died, his or her body was turned into a mummy so that the body could be used in the afterlife. It wasn't easy to enter the afterlife—everything had to be done in exactly the right way.

Ka and ba

A person was made up of two spirits, the ka and the ba. At death, the spirits were released from the body. They were reunited with the mummy when the burial tomb was shut.

The ka was the body's life force, shown by two raised arms.

The ba was the soul, or personality. It was shown as a bird.

The journey

Funerary boat

An important person was carried by boat to a tomb along the Nile. The boat might be buried, too!

Back to life

It was believed that a priest brought the mummy back to life. He did this in the "opening of the mouth" ceremony.

The pharaoh Khufu's boat was found buried next to his pyramid in 1,224 pieces.

Closing the tomb

The coffin was put in the tomb, with the Book of the Dead and all the person's possessions. The tomb was sealed shut.

Book of the Dead

Then the person traveled to the afterlife. This book, containing up to 192 spells, helped the person pass through dangers.

The heart test

Anubis weighed the person's heart against the feather of truth. If the heart was lighter, the person could enter the afterlife.

How to make a mummy

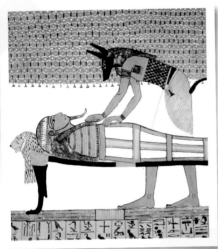

Making a mummy was a tricky process that could take up to 70 days! Here are the eight steps.

Priests

A priest performed the process, known as embalming. He wore the jackal mask of the god of embalming, Anubis.

1 Wash the body

Wash the whole body with palm wine, and rinse it with Nile water.

5 Stuff it

After 40 days, wash the body with Nile water, cover it in oil, and stuff it with leaves and linen.

6 Wrap it up

Wrap the body in layers of linen. Warning—this can take up to 15 days!

7 Tuck in jewels

Place amulets inside the wrappings to ward off evil spirits and protect the person in the afterlife.

A body had to be intact. If a limb was missing, another

The coffin that held the mummy was made to look like the dead person.

2 Remove organs

Cut down the left side of the body and remove all the organs. Leave the heart—it is needed on the journey to the afterlife.

3 Remove brain

Push a long hook up the nose to smash up the brain. Tug the brain out through the nostrils.

4 Dry the body

Stuff and cover the body with natron (a type of salt). This will dry it out completely.

8 Place in coffin

Place the mummified body in a beautifully decorated coffin.

Canopic jars

The liver, stomach, lungs, and intestines were dried out and put in canopic jars. These jars were placed in the tomb with the body. Each jar held a specific organ and was protected by one of the four sons of Horus.

had to be found. One mummy had two left legs!

Thousands of mummies from ancient Egypt—both human and animal—have been found over the centuries. More are still being found today, lying in their coffins up to 5,000 years later!

ram mummy

Tutankhamen's gold coffin

dog mummy

decorated coffin

canopic jars

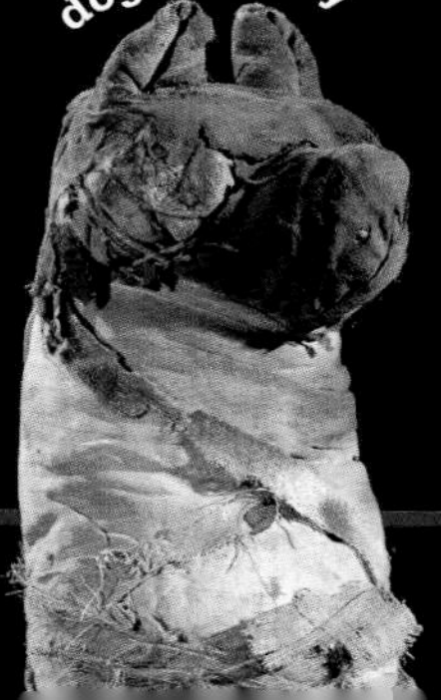

dog mummy

cat mummy

mummy

mummy

canopic jar

painted coffin

wooden coffin

coffin and mummy statue

canopic jar

unwrapped mummy

How to build a pyramid

Wealthy people were buried in amazing tombs. Nothing was more impressive than the giant pyramids. The Great Pyramid of Giza was built as the tomb for the pharaoh Khufu.

Building the Great Pyramid

The Great Pyramid was originally 481 feet (146.5 m) high. Imagine building a pyramid that big without cranes or machines! It took thousands of men 20 years to build it. No one is exactly sure how they did it.

Soldiers, farmers, and other Egyptians all helped build it.

Each stone block weighed as much as a large hippopotamus.

The stones were dragged up a ramp.

1 Foundations

Workers cut about 2.3 million huge stone blocks out of a quarry and dragged them to the site. The blocks were laid in a perfect square.

2 Building up

Teams of men used ropes and rows of logs to pull each stone up the ramp. It was hard work!

This was the tallest building in the world for nearly 4,000

Step pyramid

Djoser's step pyramid, which dates from about 2650 BCE, is the earliest known.

Bent Pyramid

The Bent Pyramid, built in about 2600 BCE by the pharaoh Snefru, is a bit crooked!

Nubian pyramids

The Nubians copied the Egyptians, building tall, thin pyramids.

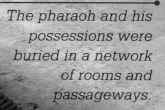

The pharaoh and his possessions were buried in a network of rooms and passageways.

3 Tomb fit for a king

In about 2566 BCE, Khufu and his belongings were placed inside. Then the pyramid was sealed shut, covered in white limestone, and topped with gold.

As the pyramid grew, the ramp had to be made steeper to reach the top.

workers' camp

years, finally overtaken by Lincoln Cathedral in the UK.

The Great Sphinx of Giza

Sprawled in front of the Pyramids of Giza, facing sunrise, lies the Great Sphinx. It has been guarding the site for 4,500 years. It is the biggest statue made out of a single piece of stone in the world. But for thousands of years it was completely buried under sand! It wasn't until 1936 that the statue was fully uncovered.

The Sphinx is gigantic. Its nose (which was destroyed

centuries ago) was once 3.3 feet (1 m) wide!

The Valley of the Kings

The pyramids were vulnerable to tomb raiders, so pharaohs began cutting hidden tombs into the hills. The area is known as the Valley of the Kings.

Royal resting place

For over 400 years (from around 1490 to 1075 BCE), pharaohs were buried in the Valley of the Kings. See the map on page 11 to find out where it is.

Entering the tombs

tomb of Ramses IV

Entrances to the next corridors were often blocked to fool tomb raiders.

corridor

The entrance

Imagine entering a long-lost tomb. The door has just been opened.

Spooky steps

Follow the dark staircase down into the hill, with only a candle for light.

Painted corridors

Walk down hallways completely covered with painted scenes.

The biggest tomb in the valley has 130 rooms—that we

Workers' village

The work in the valley took so long that the workers lived in a permanent village nearby. Freshwater had to be brought from the Nile each day.

This tomb is 290 feet (88 m) long!

This room is decorated with scenes from the Book of the Dead.

burial chamber.

A sarcophagus, a huge stone box, contained the coffin and mummy.

Treasure trove

Enter a room filled with the pharaoh's things— even 3,000-year-old bread!

The resting place

At the end, find the stone sarcophagus. Open it to discover the mummy!

Find out more

about pyramid tombs on pages 66–67.

know of. Archaeologists are still searching it for more!

Interview with an

Name: Anna Garnett
Profession: Egyptologist at the British Museum and the Manchester Museum (UK) and mummy expert

Q **Have you always been interested in ancient Egypt?**

A Absolutely, yes. When I was seven, I read a book about Tutankhamen and Howard Carter. From then on, I was obsessed with ancient Egypt. I decided that all I wanted to be was an Egyptologist.

Q **What can we learn from studying a mummy?**

A We can learn a lot about everyday life in Egypt, from what the people ate to what kinds of diseases they had. We can also learn about the process of mummification and how it changed over time.

Q **Are mummies still being found today?**

A Mummies are being found all over Egypt. In fact, archaeologists are finding some tombs that are untouched by tomb robbers.

Q **Was everyone in ancient Egypt mummified?**

A Not everyone was mummified, because the process was very expensive. Only the richest people could afford to be made into mummies. If you were poor, you were buried in the hot desert sand to dry out.

This is a cat mummy! It was mummified as an offering to the goddess Bastet.

Egyptologist

Q **Is it true that people once ate ground-up mummies as medicine?**

A Yes, it's true! In the Middle Ages, it was thought that the resin used to make mummies could cure illnesses. People collected mummies and ground them up to take as medicine. We don't do this anymore, of course!

Q **Do you have a favorite mummy?**

A My favorite is the pharaoh Seti I [below], who reigned over Egypt from about 1294 to 1279 BCE. His face is perfectly preserved, and he looks like he could wake from his long sleep at any moment.

Q **What is the weirdest mummy you've seen?**

A A princess named Henuttawy, who lived around 1050 BCE, is the weirdest. After a body was dried out, it was packed with linen and straw. Henuttawy's body was packed so full that her face exploded!

Q **How many mummies do you think were made?**

A I think there were thousands! Mummification was used from the early days of ancient Egypt right up to the end, 3,000 years later. That's a lot of mummies!

Q **If you could go back in time, what would you want to find out about ancient Egypt?**

A I would find out lots of things we don't know enough about. I would like to know how pyramids and temples were made. I would also like to see all the objects that were buried with the pharaohs.

We can see what the pharaoh Seti's face looked like.

CLEOPATRA VII

Cleopatra

The Egyptian civilization lasted for 3,000 years, only ending around 30 BCE. And it didn't end quietly. Cleopatra VII, the last pharaoh of Egypt, did everything she could to stay in power!

Cleopatra

Julius Caesar

Cleopatra was born into the ruling family of Egypt in 69 BCE. After a big family fight, she was thrown out of Egypt. Julius Caesar, the Roman emperor, was interested in Egypt, and Cleopatra knew that he was her only hope of regaining control. She returned to Egypt, hiding inside a carpet when Caesar visited Alexandria. The carpet was presented to him, and Cleopatra rolled out! Caesar fell madly in love with her, killed her enemies, and made her pharaoh.

Then Caesar was murdered in Rome. His son Octavian and a general, Mark Antony, agreed to divide the Roman Empire between themselves. Mark Antony married Cleopatra, but then Octavian attacked and defeated them. Egypt belonged to Rome, and the pharaohs never ruled again.

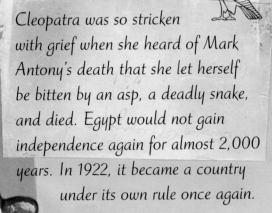

THE FINAL MOMENT

Cleopatra was so stricken with grief when she heard of Mark Antony's death that she let herself be bitten by an asp, a deadly snake, and died. Egypt would not gain independence again for almost 2,000 years. In 1922, it became a country under its own rule once again.

Glossary

afterlife
Life after death.

amulet
A jewel or ornament that is thought to bring good luck.

archaeologist
An expert who studies human history by digging things up and studying them.

asp
An Egyptian cobra.

ba
A person's soul or personality.

banquet
A big, fancy meal.

canopic jar
A container for storing one of the internal organs of a dead person.

curse
A spell that is meant to hurt someone.

death mask
In ancient Egypt, a sculpture of a dead person's face, placed on the mummy's head.

drought
A long period of dry weather that causes crops to die.

dynasty
A series of powerful rulers from the same family.

Egyptologist
An expert who studies the archaeology of ancient Egypt.

embalming
The process of treating a dead body to preserve it and prevent decay.

fertile
Full of nutrients, like soil, and good for growing crops and plants.

hieroglyphics
A system of writing used in ancient Egypt, made up of symbols and pictures that stand for words, sounds, or ideas.

ka
The body's life force.

malachite
A bright green mineral that is used in jewelry and ornaments.

mummy
A body that has been preserved and wrapped in cloth before being buried.

natron
A type of salt that was used to dry out a body during mummification.

nemes
A striped cloth that an Egyptian pharaoh wore on his head.

obelisk
A tall, pointed, four-sided stone monument.

oracle
A shrine where gods or goddesses are believed to answer questions asked by a priest or priestess.

papyrus
A tall river reed, or the paper made from it. Ancient Egyptians also made boats, rope, and baskets from papyrus.

pharaoh
The title given to the rulers of ancient Egypt.

sarcophagus
A large outer coffin made of stone.

scarab
A model of a dung beetle, used by ancient Egyptians as an amulet or ornament.

scribe
A person who wrote and copied documents by hand. Scribes were important because most Egyptians did not learn to read and write.

sidelock
A section of hair worn on the side of the head.

sphinx
An imaginary creature that has the body of a lion and the head of a man or woman.

Index

Thank you

Images

Alamy Images: 62 tl (Ancient Art & Architecture Collection Ltd.), 70 t, 71 t bg (Andrew McConnell/Robert Harding Picture Library Ltd.), 10 r bg, 11 bg (ASP GeoImaging/NASA), 37 tc (Bluered/CuboImages srl), 13 tl (David Cole), 22 bl (Everett Collection Historical), 65 r (Ian M Butterfield (Rome)), 35 tc (INTERFOTO), 15 winged beetle necklace, 53 t (Jim Henderson), 34 r, 35 bl (Mary Evans Picture Library), 28 tl, 29 cr (Michal Boubin), 31 tr (Peter Barritt/SuperStock), 37 tl (Peter Horree), 29 b (Prisma Archivo), 4 mummy, 5 mummy, 62 mummy, 63 mummy (Steve Vidler), 14 gold scarab beetle jewel, 23 bl, 38 tc, 80, (The Art Archive), 21 cbl, 42 b (Werner Forman Archive/Heritage Image Partnership Ltd.), 28 br (World History Archive/Image Asset Management Ltd.), 38 tl (Zev Radovan/BibleLandPictures.com); Anna Garnett: 72 t; AP Images: 39 tl (North Wind Picture Archives), 40 b (Paul Schemm); Art Resource/Alfredo Dagli Orti/The Art Archive: 60 tl; Bridgeman Art Library/The Weighing of the Heart against the Feather of Truth, from the Book of the Dead of the Scribe Any, c.1250 BC (painted papyrus), Egyptian 19th Dynasty (c.1297-1185 BC)/British Museum, London, UK: 58, 59; The Trustees of British Museum: 42 bg, 43 bg; Colourbox/926: cover bg gold texture, back cover bg gold texture; Corbis Images: 71 br (Asmaa Waguih/Reuters), 36 tr (Brooklyn Museum), 26 boat, 27 boat (North Carolina Museum of Art), cover main, 47 ct, 47 cb (Sandro Vannini); Dreamstime: 52 hairpin (Alain De Maximy), 16 b (Chrislofoto), 67 tl (Ian Stewart), 49 eye (Indos82), 28 bl (Krissilundgren), 70 bl (Shariff Che' Lah), 52 malachite (Tatiana Morozova), cover bg hieroglyphics, back cover bg hieroglyphics (Thirdrome); Fotolia: 54 bl (Alexandr Vasilyev), 62 br (Andrey Gorbunov), 23 tcl (Andrey Smirnov), 22 br (Andy-pix), 62 tr (Angel Simon), 11 t (BasPhoto), 57 tc (camerawithlegs), 26 bcr (Carolyn Franks), 65 wooden coffin (Cyril Comtat), 21 bl (Delmas Lehman), 22 bcr (determined), 27 tl (Detlef), 46 inset bg (dule964), 30 bg, 31 bg (ecco), 52 r, 53 l (Freesurf), 2 bg dune (Fyle), 26 br (Giuseppe Porzani), 4 hieroglyphs, 5 hieroglyphs, 8 tr, 45 border, 78 b, 79 (Igor Kovalchuk), 63 cr (Jiri Hera), 39 tc (M.Coudert), 28 bg, 29 bg (mozZz), 26 bcl (nerthuz), 43 sand (nito), 13 sand (Oleksii Sergieiev), 44 r, 45 l (Özgür Güvenç), 26 bl (Paul Fleet), 44 tl (photick2), 64 decorated coffin (PIL), 37 tr (quasarphotos), 68, 69 (ramzi hachicho), 36 palms, 37 palms, 38 palms, 39 palms (rodho), 65 coffin and mummy statue (RomainQuéré), 64 cat mummy, 65 r mummy (Sam Spiro), 63 bl (SLDigi), 56 figs (smailik), 23 bcl (Tamara Kulikova); Franck Goddio/Hilti Foundation/Christoph Gerigk: 18, 19; Getty Images: 9 tl, 15 axes and dagger, 17 t, 36 tc, 43 weapons, 47 l, 47 t, 71 bl (De Agostini), cover t (DEA PICTURE LIBRARY), 22 bcl, 31 b (G. Dagli Orti/De Agostini), 6, 7 (Kenneth Garrett/National Geographic); iStockphoto: 48 cr stone (1Photodiva), 45 hieroglyphs, 49 bird (Aaltazar), 56 dates (ac_bnphotos), 45 tr (Aerelon), 27 tr, 43 tc, 57 tr, 75 l (AmandaLewis), 52 blusher (ballycroy), 57 fish (bdspn), 48 l stone, 48 r stone, 49 cl stone (benedek), 35 tr (bigapple), 56 garlic and onion (billberryphotography), 4 board, 5 board, 12 board, 13 board, 62 wooden board, 63 wooden board (billnoll), 29 tc (Blackbeck), 33 c, 46 bg, 47 bg, 55 l (BMPix), 74 tl (bravo1954), 35 cl (brytta), 54 br (cinoby), 60 bg c, 61 bg c (danilovi), 49 tl (demarco-media), 62 bc (design56), 22 tl, 52 comb (Difydave), 21 ctl, 21 br, 63 c (DNY59), 74 b (duncan1890), 21 cb (Eduard Andras), 23 tl (EHStock), 8 bl (eishier), 56 pomegranates (eli_asenova), 48 board border, 48 board, 49 dark wood, 49 board border, 49 board (enviromantic), 29 tr (eyewave), 61 bc (Flory), 22 c (foolonthehill),

13 beer (francisblack), 20 tl (FrankvandenBergh), 26 bg, 27 bg, 76 bg, 77 bg (giac), 57 hedgehog (GlobalP), 38 tr (gmnicholas), 2 bg pyramids, 3 bg pyramids (gregobagel), 20 tc (hanoded), 22 tr (hatman12), 10 rct, 20 bg desert, 21 tr, 21 bg desert (holgs), 10 rt (Ingenui), 48 c stone, 49 cr stone (ivstiv), 21 tl (Jakich), 61 heart (januala), 34 l (jayjayoo7_com), 20 tr (jcarillet), 56 bread (JoKMedia), 23 bcr, 63 t (JoseIgnacioSoto), 30 bl (jsp), 49 l stone, 49 r stone (kapsiut), 16 border, 17 border, 40 border, 41 border, 54 border, 55 border, 74 border, 75 border (ksana-gribakina), 8 b bg, 9 b bg (Kubu), 56 b, 57 b (kwasny221), 13 magnifying glass (kyoshino), 8 tl (Linda Steward), 52 lips (Lise Gagne), 48 cl stone, 49 c stone (lucentius), 60 bg t, 61 bg t (malija), 8 br, 9 bl, 60 bc (ManuelVelasco), 35 cr (maralvar), 17 blood, 75 blood (Marek Mnich), 54 t (mit4711), 20 bg water, 21 bg water (Mlenny), 44 bl (mura), 31 tl (OKRAD), 11 b, 20 bc, 33 t, 52 bg, 53 bg (oversnap), 52 mirror (passigatti), 55 tr (PaulCowan), 29 tl (Petr Malyshev), 9 tr (Phooey), 21 ct (photonewman), 39 tr (Photoservice), 57 melons (posteriori), 26 t, 63 br, 64 canopic jars, 70 bc (powerofforever), 31 tc (Prill Medienesign & Fotografie), 56 t, 57 tl (RachelEmily), 13 bread (republica), 42 t (Richmatts), 65 t canopic jar (robyvannucci), 62 bl (rotofrank), 8 t bg, 9 t bg (sculpies), 2 b (serts), 12 t (setixela), 30 tr (sharifphoto), 23 tcr (skegbydave), 47 r (skynesher), 27 tc (small_frog), 35 br (studiocasper), 16 photo frames, 17 photo frames, 40 photo frame, 54 photo frames, 74 photo frames (subjug), 63 cl (Tarek El Sombati), 61 br (temniy), 10 rb (tenback), 60 bl, 61 bl (TerryJLawrence), 35 tl (thewizzthatwoz), 61 feather (ThomasVogel), 75 r (tunart), 36 bg, 37 bg, 38 bg, 39 bg (Ugurhan Betin), 22 cr (urbancow), 20 br (USO), 20 bl (webking); Scholastic, Inc.: 75 c inset (Karen Hood), 22 c, 45 bg, 48 t, 78 t; Science Source: 9 br, 50 fg, 51 fg, 64 l, 70 br (Brian Brake), 41 tr (Explorer), 24, 25, 53 cr (Fred Maroon), 17 bl, 36 tl (John G. Ross), 30 tl (Los Angeles County Museum), 12 mummy, 12 c, 13 mummy, 21 ctr, 60 tr, 73 (Patrick Landmann), 61 t (Robert E. Murowchick), 64 b dog mummy, 64 t dog mummy (Thierry Berrod, Mona Lisa Production); Shutterstock, Inc.: 71 t inset (BasPhoto), 21 cbr (GTS Production), 16 bg, 17 bg, 40 bg, 41 bg, 54 bg, 55 bg, 74 bg, 75 bg (inxti), 17 br, 41 br, 55 br, 75 c (Jill Battaglia), 10 l (Johan Swanepoel), 64 ram mummy, 64 painted coffin, 65 painted coffin (Jose Ignacio Soto), 23 tr (Jovanovic Dejan), 17 mosquito (jps), 67 tr (Martchan), 9 tcr (Michaela Stejskalova), 65 l mummy (Mikhail Zahranichny), 23 br (MongPro), 33 b (mountainpix), 36 b, 37 b, 38 b, 39 b (Patryk Kosmider), 65 b canopic jar (Rachelle Burnside), 22 cl (risteski goce), 50 bg, 51 bg (RoyStudio.eu), 60 br (Tatiana Grozetskaya), 41 bl (tkachuk), 53 cl (Um Sixtyfour), back cover inset, cover spine (Vladimir Wrangel), 9 tcl (Vladislav Gurfinkel), 20 c (VLADJ55), 10 rcb (Waj), cover br, 67 tc (WitR), 32, 33 bg (Zhukov Oleg); Superstock, Inc./DeAgostini: cover bl; Thinkstock: 28 tr, 29 cl (iStockphoto), 47 b (Phots.com/Getty Images); Tim Loughhead/Precision Illustration: 66, 67 b, 67 bg, 70 c, 71 c; Walters Art Museum: 1 l, 1 r, 2 t, 3 br, 14 l flask, 14 eyeliner pot, 14 stone carving, 14 baboon amulet, 14 r flask, 14 fishbowl, 14 l fish pendant, 14 r fish pendant, 14 eye amulet, 14 drinking cup, 14 glass vase, 15 god amulet, 15 cheetah necklace, 15 ibis pendant, 15 lion pendant, 15 bead, 15 double jar, 15 scarab amulet top, 15 scarab amulet bottom, 15 glass pot, 15 model boat, 15 l wooden statue, 15 c wooden statue, 15 r wooden statue, 15 wooden comb, 15 pillar amulet, 15 senet board and pieces, 15 mummy, 15 baboon mummy's coffin, 15 mummy mask, 15 l frog ring, 15 r frog ring, 15 cat mummy, 15 makeup jar, 72 b, 76 fg, 77 fg; Wikipedia: 40 t, 41 tl (AtonX), 5 b, 46 inset main (Jon Bodsworth/The Museum of Egyptian Antiquities), 16 t, 30 br.

This gorgeous ornament was found on Tutankhamen's mummy.

Answer to riddle on page 45: What a cool secret code.